BIOGRAPHIC AUDREY

BIOGRAPHIC
AUDREY

SOPHIE COLLINS

**ILLUSTRATED BY
MATT CARR**

AMMONITE
PRESS

First published 2019 by
Ammonite Press
an imprint of Guild of Master Craftsman Publications Ltd
Castle Place, 166 High Street, Lewes, East Sussex, BN7 1XU,
United Kingdom
www.ammonitepress.com

ISBN 978 1 78145 371 1

A catalogue record for this book is available from the
British Library.

Publisher: Jason Hook
Concept Design: Matt Carr
Design & Illustration: Matt Carr & Robin Shields
Editor: Jamie Pumfrey

Colour reproduction by GMC Reprographics
Printed and bound in Turkey

CONTENTS

ICONOGRAPHIC

WHEN WE CAN RECOGNIZE AN ACTOR BY
A SET OF ICONS, WE CAN ALSO RECOGNIZE
HOW COMPLETELY THAT ACTOR AND
THEIR WORK HAVE ENTERED OUR
CULTURE AND OUR CONSCIOUSNESS.

INTRODUCTION

Nearly 30 years after her death, Audrey Hepburn's many fans remain quite clear about what defines her – a stunning and very individual beauty, allied to a ladylike but sometimes offbeat style that spilled beyond her screen roles and out into her personal life. Her legacy is an image which she claimed was attainable for all women: the big shades, the little black dress, sometimes a really large hat, all worn with a careless air of just happening to be elegant. An image that is never awkward or strained but always appropriate and charming.

Behind this familiar outline, though, who was Audrey Hepburn? That's more of a conundrum than it might at first appear. All her life, she embraced the 'nothing to hide' principle when it came to her public presentation: she was open and frank in interviews, friendly with even the most difficult co-stars and modest about her achievements. And the overall impression all this affable cooperation left was that of a rather bland attractiveness, a calm and pleasant persona of whom very little criticism could be made.

But in many ways Hepburn had a challenging childhood: her father left the family when she was just eight and she didn't see him again for nearly 25 years, sparking an insecurity which would emerge in many of her adult relationships. The war overtook her teenage years, including her having to face the terrible 'Hunger Winter' in Arnhem, when she became so ill through starvation that she nearly died. When she recovered, her hopes of becoming a professional ballerina were dashed and for a while she was forced to earn a living as a chorus girl and sketch performer on the London stage – a hard career in which hundreds of girls might be competing for a handful of jobs. Although Audrey sometimes appeared to be fragile, she would never have made it through and become a star if, under the delicate exterior, there wasn't a very tough core.

"IT TOOK THE RUBBLE OF BELGIUM, AN ENGLISH ACCENT, AND AN AMERICAN SUCCESS TO LAUNCH THE STRIKING PERSONALITY THAT BEST EXEMPLIFIES OUR NEW ZEITGEIST."

—Cecil Beaton, writing in *Vogue*, 1954

To Hollywood, Audrey Hepburn was the sophisticated 'European' star; the elegant counterpoint to the luscious curves and deliberately ditsy image of Marilyn Monroe. In keeping with her image, directors found her conscientious and dutiful: not for Audrey the late arrivals or forgotten lines of many more difficult stars. And while she appeared in her fair share of stinkers and her delivery can seem oddly formal to today's audiences, in her handful of really great movies she is both luminous and touching.

And when she left it all behind, she returned to the needs of children. Above any acting ambition, Audrey had always wanted to be a mother and, having nurtured her sons to adulthood, she turned to her UNICEF ambassador role very naturally. Wherever children needed her, she was prepared to serve, often in difficult, dirty and downright heart-breaking conditions. As in all other aspects of her life, from tricky relationships to difficult roles, she didn't shirk and her strength went way beyond duty. It was maybe this willingness to see things through, in both the personal and the professional, which proved to be the hallmark of her character.

"...THAT'S THE ELEMENT X THAT PEOPLE HAVE OR THEY DON'T HAVE... SHE HAD IT. AND THERE WILL NOT BE ANOTHER."

—Billy Wilder, interviewed for *Vanity Fair*, 1999

AUDREY HEPBURN

01
LIFE

"NO-ONE EVER LOOKED LIKE HER BEFORE WORLD WAR II... YET WE RECOGNIZE THE RIGHTNESS OF THIS APPEARANCE...THE PROOF IS THAT THOUSANDS OF IMITATIONS HAVE APPEARED.

THE WOODS ARE FULL OF EMACIATED YOUNG LADIES WITH RAT-NIBBLED HAIR AND MOON-PALE FACES."

—Cecil Beaton, photographer and Oscar-winning film and theatre designer, *US Vogue*, November 1954

AUDREY HEPBURN

was born on 4 May 1929 at 48 Rue Keyenveld in Ixelles, Belgium

▼ **Commemorative plaque on the side of the building where Audrey grew up.**

CERCE D'HISTOIRE LOCALE D'IXELLES

ICI
NAQUIT
LE 4 MAI 1929
LA COMEDIENNE

AUDREY HEPBURN

Audrey Kathleen Ruston (the Hepburn, from her father's family, would be added later) was born in a comfortable suburb to the south-east of Brussels. Her mother, Baroness Ella van Heemstra, was Dutch and came from a well-off family of minor aristocrats; her father, Joseph Ruston, although often identified as Irish, seems to have had mainly English antecedents. It was a second marriage for both her parents, who had met in Batavia (now Jakarta, Indonesia), then part of the colonial Dutch East Indies, but had moved to Brussels. Audrey had two half-brothers from her mother's earlier marriage but was the only child her parents had together.

BELGIUM

Also born in Brussels: ▶
Jacques Brel (1929–78)
**The hugely popular French
singer and composer was
born on 9 April 1929, just a
month before Audrey.**

1929 IN FILM

By the time that Audrey Hepburn was born, talking pictures were quickly becoming the norm in Hollywood, winning out over silent movies, which were looking increasingly dated. The same year saw the first Academy awards – and also the first university course in film.

END OF AN ERA

Pandora's Box, directed by G. W. Pabst and starring Louise Brooks, is released in Germany on 30 January. A powerful melodrama, it will be one of the last gasps of the great silent movie tradition.

THE MARX BROTHERS

Chico, Groucho (above), Harpo and Zeppo appear together in the first Marx Brothers full-length feature film, *The Cocoanuts*.

"HOT DOGS!"

AWARD WINNER

MGM release the first original musical. *The Broadway Melody* premieres at Grauman's Chinese Theater in Hollywood on 1 February. It will be the first sound film to win the Academy's Best Picture award (in 1930).

MICKEY SPEAKS

The Karnival Kid, Disney's ninth cartoon featuring Mickey Mouse, uses Walt Disney's own voice to utter Mickey's first spoken words "Hot dogs!"

THE START OF THE 'TALKIES'

His Glorious Night marks the beginning of the end of the career of romantic silent movie lead John Gilbert (below). His first 'talkie' reveals his squeaky, high-pitched voice.

ACADEMY AWARDS

The first Academy Awards ceremony is held at the Hollywood Roosevelt Hotel on 16 May; 12 award statuettes are presented at a private dinner with just 270 guests, who have each paid $5 to attend.

BOX OFFICE HIT

King Vidor directs *Hallelujah!*, the first full-length talkie with an all-black cast. He puts up half the budget himself and foregoes his own fee. The risk pays off and it is a big box office success.

THE BIRTH OF COLOUR

On With the Show, the first '100 per cent Natural Color, Talking, Singing, Dancing Picture' opens in New York on 28 May.

DUBBING

Alfred Hitchcock releases *Blackmail,* the first full-length British 'talkie'. A silent version is also released, as many cinemas still don't have the technology to play sound. In one of the first instances of movie dubbing, the actress Joan Barry speaks the lines of the female lead, Anny Ondra.

FILM SCHOOL

The University of Southern California founds its School of Cinematic Arts, the first university in the US to offer a BA in film. Frank Capra and Greta Garbo are among its early guest lecturers.

GRANDMOTHER
**Elbrig
Wilhelmina
Henriette van
Asbeck**
(1873–1939)

GRANDFATHER
**Aarnoud Johan,
Baron van
Heemstra**
(1871–1957)

MOTHER
**Ella, Baroness
van Heemstra**
(1900–84)

**Audrey
Kathleen
Ruston
(Hepburn)**
(1929–93)

HALF-BROTHER
**Alexander
Quarles
van Ufford**
(1920–79)

HALF-BROTHER
**Ian Quarles
van Ufford**
(1924–2010)

MEET THE HEPBURNS

It's a surprise, looking at Audrey Hepburn's immediate family tree, that the surname 'Hepburn' doesn't appear anywhere. But in 1939 her father, previously Joseph Ruston, became Joseph Hepburn-Ruston, believing that the name was inherited through his paternal grandmother. However, it seems more likely that Isabella Ruston, née Hepburn, was actually his grandfather's first wife whereas it was the second who was Joseph's mother.

THE HEPBURN NAME

What made the 'Hepburn' name desirable? It enabled Audrey's father to claim indirect, but still impressive, descent from Mary, Queen of Scots, whose third husband, the Earl of Bothwell, was John Hepburn. Audrey never seems to have questioned the story: by the time she was working as a chorus girl in London, after the war, she had lost the 'Ruston', and her surname had become simply 'Hepburn'.

GRANDMOTHER
Anna Catherina Wels
(b.1868)

GRANDFATHER
Victor John George Ruston
(c.1831–c.1889)

FATHER
Joseph Victor Anthony Ruston
(1900–84)

HUSBAND
Mel Ferrer
(1917–2008)

HUSBAND
Andrea Dotti
(1938–2007)

LONG-TERM PARTNER
Robert Wolders
(1936–2018)

SON
Sean Ferrer
(b.1960)

SON
Luca Dotti
(b.1970)

LIFE

EARLY LIFE...

Born to parents with very different backgrounds and expected to fit in with all kinds of situations almost from birth, Audrey had an unsettled early life. As an adult she would blame her father's desertion for her own inability to trust relationships, but looking at the events of her early life, it seems unsurprising that she would always crave love and continuity. Moving from Belgium to England to the Netherlands, she adapted, chameleon-like, to a whole range of circumstances.

1939 On the outbreak of war, Ella decides that it will be safer if she and Audrey return to Ella's homeland. Audrey's father finds a place for her on one of the last flights out of England to the Netherlands. She will not see him again for almost 25 years.

Ella and Audrey set up home in Arnhem, where Ella's family live.

Audrey has to re-learn Dutch after five years away – English has become her first language.

1929 Audrey is born on 4 May to Ella van Heemstra and Joseph Ruston. The family are based in Brussels. Audrey has two older half-brothers, Alexander and Ian, from Ella's first marriage.

1938 Ella and Joseph's divorce is finalized.

1934 While her family move around, five-year-old Audrey is sent to boarding school in England. She spends holidays with an English family and, after an initial struggle, learns to speak English fluently.

1936 Joseph walks out on the family. Audrey is deeply affected by his departure and spends the rest of her life looking for stability in her relationships.

Audrey starts dance lessons, beginning a lifelong love affair with ballet.

1935 Ella and Joseph actively recruit for the British Union of Fascists and, in May, have a meeting with Adolf Hitler in Munich, Germany. Both will recant before war begins, but these events will cause Audrey future embarrassment.

Second World War

1940

Sadler's Wells Ballet perform in Arnhem on the same day as Germany invades.

Queen Wilhelmina flees to England, from where she re-forms a government. A Dutch-speaking station is set up by the BBC, and the queen urges her citizens to resist the Nazis.

Ella registers Audrey in school as Edda van Heemstra, to avoid using an English name under German occupation.

1941

Audrey begins to study ballet seriously at the Arnhem Conservatory of Music and Dance.

Privations begin for civilians under the occupation. Food is scarce and families are allowed to heat only one room at home.

1942

Ella's brother Otto is executed by the Nazis during reprisals for underground activities.

Audrey's half-brother Alexander goes underground; her other half-brother, Ian, is taken to Berlin to work in a munitions factory until the end of the war.

Audrey and Ella move from the centre of Arnhem to the suburb of Velp to live with Ella's recently widowed father.

1946

Ella moves the family to Amsterdam, where Audrey enrols with the most famous name in Dutch ballet, Sonia Gaskell.

1945

Picked up on the street, Audrey is forced onto a lorry with other girls, bound for a German labour camp, but escapes. She hides at home for the month with her family until Liberation comes on 4 May, by which time she weighs only 90 pounds (41 kg).

1944

The Hunger Winter and the loss of the Battle of Arnhem drives the population of Arnhem to desperate straits, and many starve. Audrey is so malnourished that she has to stop dancing.

1943

Audrey works in the Resistance movement, acting as a courier. She also holds clandestine dance performances to raise money for the Resistance.

DANCING QUEEN

On the night of 9 May 1940, Audrey attended a performance of *Façade* in Arnhem. The dancers were the Sadler's Wells Ballet company, and the prima ballerina was Audrey's idol, the 19-year-old Margot Fontey. However, unnerved by the gunfire from the nearby frontline, the company departed early. The very next day, German forces marched into Arnhem. Over the years of privation that followed, Audrey still danced when she could. In 1947, she moved to London with her mother to take up a place at the prestigious ballet school run by Marie Rambert. Long-limbed, she had remained very slight, but had grown too tall for a professional and when a selected group of students set off on a tour of Australia in the summer of 1948, she wasn't chosen to accompany them. It was time to look for an alternative career.

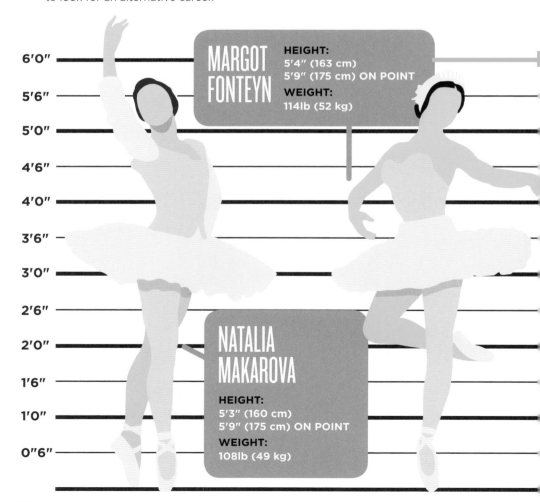

6'0"

5'6"

5'0"

4'6"

4'0"

3'6"

3'0"

2'6"

2'0"

1'6"

1'0"

0"6"

MARGOT FONTEYN

HEIGHT:
5'4" (163 cm)
5'9" (175 cm) ON POINT

WEIGHT:
114lb (52 kg)

NATALIA MAKAROVA

HEIGHT:
5'3" (160 cm)
5'9" (175 cm) ON POINT

WEIGHT:
108lb (49 kg)

RULES ARE RULES

Rules in the ballet world of the 1940s were even stricter than they are today: a ballerina couldn't be too heavy for her partner to lift, nor could she loom over him when she was standing on point. Audrey was certainly light enough – she weighed even less than Margot Fonteyn – but she was at least three inches too tall, and her size 9 feet meant that, standing on point, she was substantially taller than most of her potential partners. Forty years later, even after ballet body norms had broadened out a little, Sylvie Guillem, legendary star of both the Paris Opera Ballet and London's Royal Ballet, was heavier than Hepburn had been, but she was still a full inch shorter.

SYLVIE GUILLEM

HEIGHT:
5'6" (168 cm)
5'10" (178 cm) ON POINT
WEIGHT:
121lb (55 kg)

AUDREY HEPBURN

HEIGHT:
5'7" (170 cm)
5'11" (180 cm) ON POINT
WEIGHT:
110lb (50 kg)

6'0"
5'6"
5'0"
4'6"
4'0"
3'6"
3'0"
2'6"
2'0"
1'6"
1'0"
0"6"

GETTING THE LOOK

Tall and thin, Audrey was a natural clothes horse. She loved clothes, too, so when, in the lead-up to the 1953 film *Sabrina*, she was told she would need to wear couture for the scenes after her Cinderella character's transformation, she was delighted. Hubert de Givenchy, one of the newest couturiers, was equally pleased to hear that Miss Hepburn wanted an appointment – he had always admired Katherine Hepburn's style. But he opened the door to a gamine figure wearing Capri trousers, flat slippers and the flat-brimmed hat of a Venetian gondolier. However, the misunderstanding led to a style collaboration that would last until Audrey's death.

WHO WAS HUBERT?

Aristocratic, elegant and an imposing 6 feet 6 inches (198 cm), Hubert de Givenchy was known in the couture world as 'Le Grand'. At the time he first met Audrey Hepburn, he was 26 to her 22, and had opened his studio just two years earlier. In 1957, Hepburn – unpaid – would become the first ever 'face' of a scent when he launched *L'interdit*, which has sold successfully ever since.

THE GIVENCHY TREATMENT

Givenchy explained he was too busy to make couture for *Sabrina*; Audrey riposted that she would be happy with ready-made clothes. She was both slim and tall enough for the model's clothes to fit her – and from that point on, if a film she was appearing in had a modern setting, Givenchy would dress her for it.

"I ALWAYS RESPECTED AUDREY'S TASTE. SHE WAS NOT LIKE OTHER MOVIE STARS IN THAT SHE LIKED SIMPLICITY."

—Hubert de Givenchy, interview with Drusilla Beyfus, *The Daily Telegraph*, 2015

AUDREY

AUDREY'S SIMPLE STYLE

Even in the early days, Audrey wore a preponderance of black.

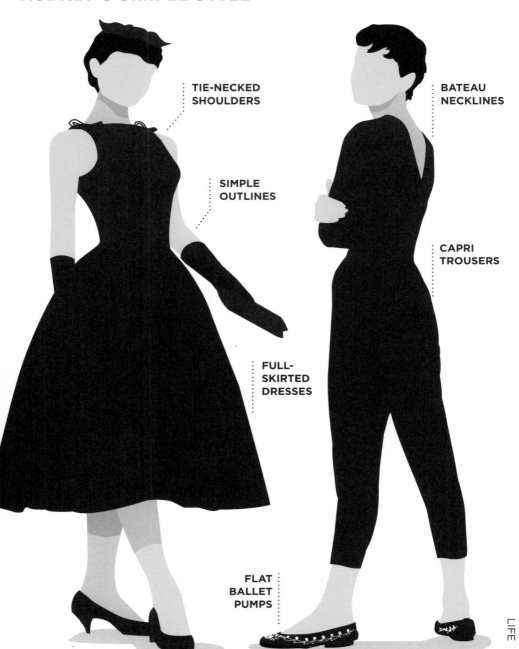

TIE-NECKED
SHOULDERS

BATEAU
NECKLINES

SIMPLE
OUTLINES

CAPRI
TROUSERS

FULL-
SKIRTED
DRESSES

FLAT
BALLET
PUMPS

BECOMING A STAR

When the war finished, Audrey had just turned 16 – and shortly afterwards the long-term effects of strain and malnutrition caught up with her and she became very ill. After a spell in hospital in Amsterdam she spent a brief time studying ballet with the country's foremost teacher, Sonia Gaskell, before moving to London with her mother in 1947.

1951

Takes a part in *Secret People* and is offered a part in *Monte Carlo Baby*. Auditions for the lead part in *Gigi* on Broadway in New York. It premieres in November and is an immediate hit.

1947

Arrives in London and starts studying at Marie Rambert's ballet school.

1950

Appears in *Sauce Tartare* and makes a film appearance playing a cigarette girl in *Laughter in Paradise*. Becomes engaged to James Hanson, heir to a trucking fortune.

1948

Told she is too tall to be a professional ballerina. Auditions for a chorus girl role in the musical *High Button Shoes* and wins a place.

1949

Her part is increased in her next show, *Sauce Piquante*. Augments income by doing floor shows at Ciro's nightclub.

1952

Roman Holiday starts shooting in June and completes in September. Audrey begins to tour with *Gigi* in October. She breaks off her engagement.

1963

Is offered the part of Eliza in the film of *My Fair Lady* and is paid $1 million for taking on the role. On its release in 1964, it's a major hit, but critics agree Audrey is miscast.

1953

With the release of *Roman Holiday*, she becomes a major star. In September, filming starts on *Sabrina*, directed by Billy Wilder.

1960

Gives birth to her first child, Sean. The following year *Breakfast at Tiffany's* and *The Children's Hour* are released.

1954

Plays the lead in *Ondine* on Broadway opposite Mel Ferrer; the couple marry in September. She wins the Academy Award for Best Actress, for *Roman Holiday*.

1958

In rapid succession, stars in *The Nun's Story*, *Green Mansions* and *The Unforgiven*. Thrown by a horse in the latter, she breaks her back and shortly afterwards suffers a miscarriage.

LOOKING FOR LOVE

Audrey's rather chaste and untouchable public image wasn't really reflected by her romantic history. She had plenty of relationships, a number of them overlapping with her two marriages. She later said that she had stayed in both of the latter far too long, for the sake of a semblance of family stability for her two sons. After a life of ups and downs, her 12-year relationship with the Dutch actor Robert Wolders seems finally to have provided the emotional safe haven she had been looking for.

● **Lovers**

● **Engagement**

● **Husbands**

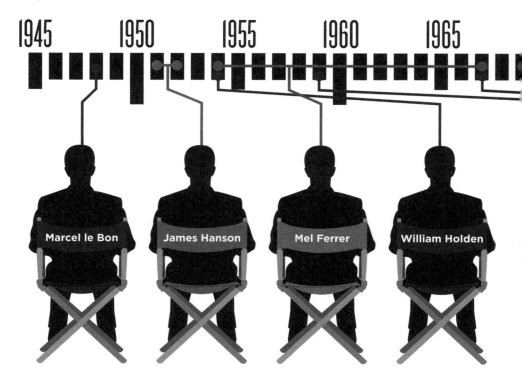

1945   1950   1955   1960   1965

Marcel le Bon

James Hanson

Mel Ferrer

William Holden

A French singer who appeared with Audrey in *High Button Shoes*.

After multiple postponements of the wedding day, their engagement was broken off in 1952.

Audrey appeared with the actor in *Ondine* and *War and Peace.* They married in 1954 and divorced in 1967.

The actor was one of Audrey's co-stars in *Sabrina*.

1981–1993
ROBERT WOLDERS

The Dutch actor was Audrey's soul mate and partner from 1981 until her death in 1993.

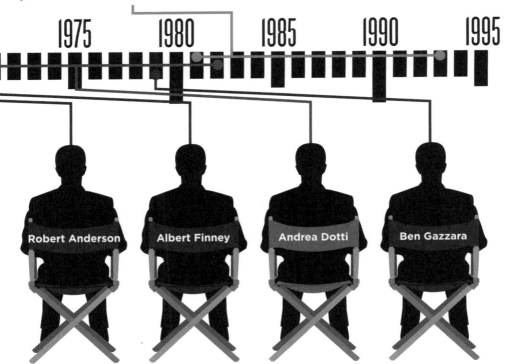

1975   1980   1985   1990   1995

Robert Anderson

Anderson was the playwright and scriptwriter on *The Nun's Story*.

Albert Finney

Audrey's co-star in *Two for the Road*.

Andrea Dotti

An Italian psychiatrist and Roman socialite. The couple married in 1969 and divorced in 1982.

Ben Gazzara

Audrey's co-star in *Bloodline*.

SMOKING HOT!

The cigarette holder in *Breakfast at Tiffany's* wasn't just for show. Hepburn was a heavy smoker all her adult life, having started at the end of the war, at around 16 years old. She continued through the 1970s and 1980s, long after smoking was fashionable. Despite her often-fragile health, at stressful times she could get through up to three packs a day – the wardrobe department on *The Nun's Story* allegedly complained that they couldn't get the tarry smell out of her weighty nun's habits. She tended to use a holder in real life (her mother gave her one and tried to get her to limit her daily consumption to just six cigarettes), but her choice of brand was decidedly heavy duty.

21 NON SMOKING

7

MOVIES IN WHICH AUDREY SMOKED

$10,000

The amount paid – each – to film stars Gary Cooper, Joan Crawford, Spencer Tracy and Clark Gable to promote Lucky Strike cigarettes in 1938.

"GOLD FLAKE" CIGARETTES

10 CIGARETTES

WHICH BRAND DID AUDREY SMOKE?

Gold Flake, switching to Kent in the 1970s.

HOW MANY A DAY?

JUDY GARLAND
Allegedly (studio bosses encouraged it to keep her weight down).

80

AUDREY HEPBURN / BETTE DAVIS

60

KATHERINE HEPBURN
Until she quit, cold turkey!

ELIZABETH TAYLOR
Until 1975 (when she was diagnosed with lung problems); post-1975 she still smoked, but sporadically.

40

MARILYN MONROE

10

Marilyn was a sporadic smoker, this was a heavy day.

LIFE AS A STAR

By the time *My Fair Lady* became a hit, in the mid-1960s, Audrey's first marriage only had three years to run. She and Mel Ferrer had been drifting apart for some years, and their difficulties were exacerbated by the fact that she had long outstripped him in fame and success. In the drift to divorce, though, she found the house that would act as her stronghold for the rest of her life.

1969 She marries Andrea Dotti, an Italian psychiatrist, and moves to Rome, to an apartment on Ponte Vittorio.

1968 She begins to spend increasing amounts of time staying with friends in Rome while her son Sean is in school.

1965 Audrey finds the house, La Paisible, where she will live, on and off, for the rest of her life, in Tolochenaz, Switzerland. She buys it independently of Ferrer, to whom she is still married.

She travels to Paris, where she films *How to Steal a Million* with Peter O'Toole.

1967 At the end of the year, Audrey and Mel Ferrer separate for good.

1966 She films *Two for the Road*, which is mainly shot in the south of France, including interiors in St Tropez, and has an affair with her co-star, Albert Finney. The film's wardrobe department updates her image steering her into outfits by designers such as Mary Quant and Courrèges.

1966/7 The Ferrers discuss building a home on the Spanish coast, near to Marbella, where Mel is filming. *Wait Until Dark*, Audrey's first suspense film, in which she plays the blind heroine, is filmed in New York and Hollywood.

1970
Her son with Dotti, Luca, is born after a difficult pregnancy involving some months of near-complete bedrest at La Paisible.

1971
Audrey makes four commercials for a Japanese wig company, Varie, for which she is paid $100,000. She also appears in a UNICEF documentary, representing Italy.

1976
Audrey makes her first film in some years, *Robin and Marian*, opposite Sean Connery, who will become a lifelong friend. It is filmed near Pamplona in Spain.

1979
Bloodline, a widely panned thriller, is filmed in Munich with Audrey in the lead. It is one of her few real flops.

1989
She plays her final film role, a cameo in *Always*, directed by Steven Spielberg.

1984
Audrey's mother, Ella, dies at La Paisible, after living there for the preceding few years.

1980
After filing for divorce in Rome, Audrey flies to Los Angeles to film *They All Laughed* with Peter Bogdanovich. She has the same co-star as in *Bloodline*, Ben Gazzara, with whom she has a relationship, but the film, again, is a flop. She meets Robert Wolders, a Dutch actor who will be her companion for the rest of her life.

AUDREY'S DEATH

DATE:
20 JANUARY
1993

AGE:
63 YEARS
OLD

Audrey Hepburn died at her home, La Paisible in Switzerland, having been diagnosed with cancer less than three months earlier. It had begun in her appendix, where it had remained unspotted until it spread to her colon. She spent Christmas happily with her sons and Robert Wolders, enjoying her garden and summoning friends to say goodbye. With characteristic thoughtfulness, she chose remembrance gifts for each of them.

TIFFANY'S TRIBUTE

On the day her death was announced, Tiffany's placed her photograph in their shop window with a caption, quoting from the song 'Moon River', written for her by Henry Mancini:

'There's such a lot of world to see.
We're after the same rainbow's end,
waitin' 'round the bend,
my Huckleberry friend,
Moon River, and me...'

—Audrey Hepburn,
our Huckleberry friend,
1929–1993

AUDREY HEPBURN

02
WORLD

"I THINK THAT THAT'S WHAT LIFE IS ALL ABOUT, ACTUALLY, ABOUT CHILDREN AND FLOWERS."

–Audrey Hepburn speaking about her TV series, *Gardens of the World*, shown posthumously in 1993

ARNHEM AND THE HUNGER WINTER

Audrey and her mother Ella went to live in the Netherlands on the outbreak of war because Ella feared that London would be heavily bombed. In one way she was right, but the choice of Arnhem, where Ella's family lived, was unfortunate. Occupation overnight in May 1940 by the Germans, followed by increased Dutch resistance, led to both a brutal regime and an all-round scarcity of supplies. In October 1944 the 'Hunger Winter' arrived, the harshest in memory. Bad weather added to the shortage of food, and combined with a failed attempt by the British to retake Arnhem, which led to the forced evacuation of the whole town, starvation became widespread. The Liberation finally came on Audrey's 16th birthday.

SEPTEMBER 1944 ARNHEM

Operation Market Garden, an Allied attempt to recapture five key bridges from Nazi forces, is launched. In the case of Arnhem's bridge, immortalized in the movie *A Bridge Too Far*, it fails. The town's civilian population of

90,000

is forcibly evacuated as a result, leading to the deaths of an estimated

5,000

civilians.

= 100 people

FEBRUARY 1945 AMSTERDAM

Adults in Amsterdam – where some food was still available – were subsisting on rations of

580

calories per day.

4 MAY 1945 ARNHEM

Audrey's family emerge from the cellar, where they've been hiding during the heavy bombardment over the previous month, to find that English troops have arrived in Arnhem.

> "WE ATE NETTLES AND EVERYONE TRIED TO COOK GRASS, ONLY I COULDN'T STAND IT."

—Audrey Hepburn, speaking of the Hunger Winter

**The Siegfried Line
– German defensive
line during the 1930s.**

Allied route

Food supplies quickly became a problem in
Holland as winter arrived. Townspeople began
to travel into the country, visiting farms to
try to exchange valuables for food, but soon
there wasn't enough to go around even in the
countryside. People boiled up tulip bulbs to
make 'onion' soup; when even those ran out,
they ate weeds.

Velp, the village/
suburb where Audrey
and her mother live
in her grandfather's
house. Slightly to the
west of Arnhem, it
escapes the forced
evacuation of 1944.

AMSTERDAM

NETHERLANDS

ARNHEM

ROTTERDAM

EINDHOVEN

GERMANY

BELGIUM

IN REVUE

After the war, people were ready to start enjoying life again, especially public entertainments. By the start of the 1950s in London, musical theatre was thriving. Sometimes shows revolved around a storyline, sometimes they were more like old-style music hall, incorporating skits, comedy acts and songs. When, in 1949, it became clear that Audrey didn't have a professional future in ballet, she did a brief turn in musical theatre as a chorus girl. Despite her lack of curves – which were usually considered a necessity on the chorus line – and the fact her ballet training didn't help much with the 'hoofing' that was required on stage, she seemed to attract the lion's share of the attention in all three of the shows she appeared in – *High Button Shoes*, *Sauce Tartare* and *Sauce Piquante*.

SHOWS
IN 1949/50
Fewer than 150 performances was considered a flop

Cowboy Casanova
Theatre Royal, Stratford — 8 — | FLOP

Golden City
Adelphi Theatre — 140

Dear Miss Phoebe
Phoenix Theatre — 283

Sauce Tartare
Cambridge Theatre — 433

Carousel
Theatre Royal, Drury Lane — 566

Blue for a Boy
His Majesty's Theatre — 664

By Audrey's third show, she was doing small skits as well as chorus line dance numbers and this was reflected in her weekly pay.

10 places available

1,000 girls applied to dance in the chorus line in *High Button Shoes*

High Button Shoes (1948)	£8 10s	
Sauce Tartare (1949)	£10	
Sauce Piquante (1950)	£15	

DUB STAR

When Jack Warner, the president of Warner Bros., cast Audrey Hepburn as Eliza in the film of *My Fair Lady*, he picked her over Julie Andrews, despite the fact that Andrews had been a huge hit when she played the part on Broadway. This went largely unquestioned as Hepburn was the established movie star and better for the box office. But there was a drawback: Audrey's singing voice, though pretty, wasn't very strong. The solution lay with Marni Nixon, whose vibrant soprano was the unacknowledged answer for directors when their leading ladies' voices proved unequal to the job.

WHO KNEW?

Dubbing artists were traditionally contracted with gagging clauses to prevent them taking any credit for the singing in 'their' films. In 1964, just in advance of the release of *My Fair Lady*, *Time* magazine broke the vow of silence about the 'secret' voice in the film.

EARNINGS

Marni Nixon's earnings were far from stellar. For example, for the substantial amount of work she did on *The King & I*, she received a flat fee of

$420

In comparison, Audrey's fee per movie in the 1960s was around:

$1 million

Marni finally appeared on screen as a singing nun in 1965 with Julie Andrews in *The Sound of Music,* although she only had a small part with a couple of lines in the song 'How Do You Solve a Problem Like Maria?'

HOW MUCH MARNI?

Marni Nixon was a successful opera singer and a lifelong voice and singing coach. Her involvement in films varied though – in *Gentlemen Prefer Blondes*, for example, she simply hit a few unreachable high notes in a single song for Marilyn Monroe. Natalie Wood, though, believed her own voice would be used in *West Side Story* and was devastated when she discovered that Nixon had covered her for the whole film. Other actresses were more phlegmatic: both Audrey and Deborah Kerr accepted Nixon's superior voice dubbed over their own efforts.

1953 🚫 = Gagging clause
GENTLEMEN PREFER BLONDES
MARILYN MONROE

Just the high notes in 'Diamonds are a Girl's Best Friend'

1956 🚫
THE KING & I
DEBORAH KERR

4 SONGS

1961 🚫
WEST SIDE STORY
NATALIE WOOD

7 SONGS

1964 🚫
MY FAIR LADY
AUDREY HEPBURN

10 SONGS

WORLD

HOLLYWOOD ON THE TIBER

That Hepburn's first big hit was filmed in Rome, rather than on a back lot of the Paramount studio in Hollywood, was thanks to the presence of Cinecittà, the iconic studio located just 15 miles south-east of the city. Founded by the Fascist government in the 1930s as a European answer to Hollywood, it swiftly became popular with the international market after the war. Filming cost less in Italy, the weather tended to be reliable and Rome itself was just up the road for location filming. While it specialized in sword-and-sandals epics, the iconic Italian director Federico Fellini would also make its name as the centre for neo-realism, with movies such as *La Dolce Vita* marking a golden age in Italian film.

OPENED 28 APRIL 1937 BY BENITO MUSSOLINI

The date was chosen because, in legend, it was the founding day of the city of Ancient Rome.

Hepburn made

2 MOVIES

at Cinecittà – *Roman Holiday* (1953) and *War and Peace* (1956).

279
NUMBER OF FILMS MADE IN CINECITTÀ'S FIRST SIX YEARS

100
ACRES: OVERALL AREA OF CINECITTÀ

19
NUMBER OF STAGES

112,000
SQUARE FEET

Size of the studio's outdoor tank for filming on or in water

COSTLY CLEO

Of Hepburn's Cinecittà movies, *Roman Holiday* was a modestly budgeted hit with well-behaved stars which made Paramount good profits. Even the more costly *War and Peace*, in which she starred in 1956, came in at just under $6 million. At the other end of the scale was *Cleopatra*, the Richard Burton/Elizabeth Taylor spectacular which almost bankrupted its American studio, 20th Century-Fox. Taylor's uncertain health forced the move to Cinecittà from an English film set well into shooting. This meant the sets had to be entirely remade in Italy – including a Roman forum that was three times the size of the original.

ITTA'

FOR YOUR EYES ONLY

Sunglasses were a key part of the Hepburn look: she credited their role herself, saying, "My look is attainable. Women can look like Audrey Hepburn by flipping out their hair, buying the large sunglasses, and the little sleeveless dresses...". She underestimated the qualities she brought to the look though. In her private life, she often wore quite plain sunglasses, although they were usually outsized; in the movies, however, she would be more experimental.

BREAKFAST AT TIFFANY'S

MANHATTAN (OLIVER GOLDSMITH, 1961)

The oversized sunglasses, often rumoured to be Ray-bans, were in fact manufactured by Oliver Goldsmith, who was also favoured by Jackie Kennedy, Grace Kelly and Cary Grant.

HOW TO STEAL A MILLION

BUDE (OLIVER GOLDSMITH, 1965)

Four years later, the white wraparound style marked the coming of age of the 1960s, with a nod to increasingly space-age styling.

WHITE OVALS (OLIVER GOLDSMITH, 1967)

This was the first movie in which Audrey wore modern fashion from designers other than Givenchy, ranging from Mary Quant to André Courrèges. In it, she wore a pair of huge Goldsmith sunglasses...

BLACK WRAPAROUNDS (ANDRÉ COURRÈGES, 1967)

... but also accessories from the then-cutting edge Courrèges, famous for his flat white 'space' boots...

FUTURISTIC YELLOW VISOR (ANDRÉ COURRÈGES, 1967)

...and one frankly impractical, yellow, visor-styled pair.

Both Audrey Hepburn and Grace Kelly had well-earned reputations for sophistication, but in quite different ways. Hepburn's gamine looks and effervescent energy contrasted strongly with Kelly's patrician blonde beauty and cool delivery. Both maintained pristine reputations, in spite of on-set affairs conducted at a time when they were frowned upon.

AUDREY HEPBURN

TYPECASTING?

Funny but poignant romances, often with a bittersweet edge.

BACKGROUND

Low-level European aristocracy, impoverished by the Second World War. Audrey had to earn her own living from her teens and was actively encouraged to perform.

27 MOVIES

63 YEARS

Academy Award: **Best actress, _Roman Holiday_, 1954**

41 YEARS

MOVIE CAREER: 1948–89

BORN: 1929   DIED: 1993

GRACE KELLY

Kelly's short career in movies ended when she married a bona fide prince – Rainier of Monaco, head of one of the world's smallest fiefdoms – while still in her 20s. Hepburn continued to act, her career gradually tailing off as family and charity interests took centre stage.

TYPECASTING?

The archetypal cool, collected Hitchcock blonde (she starred in three of his movies: *Rear Window, Dial M for Murder* and *To Catch a Thief*).

BACKGROUND

Well-off Irish-American family from Philadelphia, with a strong sporting streak (her father was an Olympian), and a low tolerance of the stage. Grace had to negotiate her way into show business.

52 YEARS

11 MOVIES

Academy Award: Best actress, *The Country Girl*, 1955

MOVIE CAREER: 1951 – 56

BORN: 1929 DIED: 1982

5 YEARS

1953 CROPPED WITH A FRINGE

When, in *Roman Holiday*, Princess Ann goes to the barbers and has around 18 inches (50 cm) of hair chopped off, it's a sign of her liberation from convention.

1957 PIXIE CROP

A wide variety of hairstyles in *Funny Face* was trumped by the pixie crop. The images were cut out of magazines and taken to the hairdressers by millions of women, few of whom, unfortunately for them, had Audrey's eyes or cheekbones.

CUTTING EDGE

In the chorus line, it had been Audrey's eyes that got her attention; as she went from starlet to star, though, her hairstyles became the most imitated, from the gamine crop to the 1960s' beehive and the 1970s' loose perm. As she grew older, her hair got simpler, mostly pulled straight back from her face, allowing her bone structure to take centre stage.

1961 CHIGNON

High-piled styles for 'occasions' were still in fashion at the turn of the 1960s; Holly's casual, wispy chignon in *Breakfast at Tiffany's* caught the look perfectly.

1963 BEEHIVE

Audrey wore the beehive both in life and on film: by the early 1960s, brushed back and sprayed in place, it had become almost universal.

1970s MID-LENGTH, PULLED BACK

After a short flirtation with short-and-curly, the style Audrey favoured through her 40s and 50s tended to be mostly mid-length and pulled back, ballerina-fashion.

PROP, NOT PET

Audrey kept pet dogs throughout her life, but the most famous of her pets was not actually a pet at all. In *Green Mansions*, the movie directed by Audrey's husband Mel Ferrer, she had to become a wild jungle girl, forever accompanied by her equally wild pet deer. Deer need time to bond. So MGM bought a doe fawn, Pippin, at Jungleland, a petting zoo in Los Angeles. The on-set animal trainer encouraged Audrey to take Pippin home to teach her to follow the actor.

4
weeks

The age at which Pippin came to live with Audrey

2.5
months

The amount of time Pippin lived with the Ferrers

MR FAMOUS

Only one of Audrey's real pets made it onto the screen; Mr Famous, her first Yorkshire terrier and a present from Ferrer, briefly appears with his mistress in the dramatic train scene in *Funny Face*. His successor, Assam of Assam, never acted with her, and by the time she was living full-time at La Paisible, where she owned a number of Jack Russell terriers, she had largely retired from acting herself.

WHAT BECAME OF PIPPIN?

Pippin, named Ip for short, was photographed with Audrey everywhere. Both had doe eyes and long legs, but Ip raised the biggest sensation when she was spotted accompanying Audrey to the supermarket. No records exist of what happened to Ip when filming was over, but the Ferrers did not keep her; she was probably returned to Jungleland.

03
WORK

"SHE HAD ONE SKIRT, ONE BLOUSE, ONE PAIR OF SHOES AND A BERET, BUT SHE HAD FOURTEEN SCARVES. WHAT SHE DID WITH THEM, WEEK BY WEEK, YOU WOULDN'T BELIEVE."

—Nikolas Dana, dancer in *High Button Shoes* – and one of the first to spot Hepburn's innate sense of style

MAKING IT ON BROADWAY

Myth has it that Audrey was 'discovered' on the French Riviera during the filming of *Monte Carlo Baby*. The septuagenarian French author Colette, by then in a wheelchair, spotted the young star dancing and asked her carer to stop, exclaiming, "Voila, there is my Gigi!" And, equally famously, Audrey is said to have turned down the offer, saying, "But Madame, I can't act." After some negotiation, though, the deal was done and Audrey was launched in her first stage hit.

BECOM

3

Inexperience made Audrey an uncertain performer, and she was fired and rehired three times before opening night – when she became an immediate hit.

$500

Hepburn's earnings per week

POOR PROJECTION

Audrey had never acted on stage and had to learn to project her voice

Audrey's performance was such a hit that within a week, the marquee of the Fulton Theater, where she was appearing, was changed:

GIGI
With
AUDREY HEPBURN

BECAME →

AUDREY HEPBURN
In
GIGI

NG GIGI

15 POUNDS (7 kg)

To her director's horror, Audrey had gained 15 pounds (7 kg) while crossing the Atlantic by liner. On arrival in America, she was put on a diet of steak tartare and lost the weight in two weeks – the only time she was ever required to diet.

RISQUÉ ROOTS

By the 1950s, Colette was the 'grande dame' of literature, féted all over her native France for the novels and short stories she had been producing since her early 20s. Young girls emerging into adulthood (often guided by older men) were a staple of her writing and when she published *Gigi*, it was the unvarnished account of a young girl in training to become a courtesan. Turned into a play by Anita Loos, the American actress-turned-playwright who had herself been considered risqué in the past, *Gigi* needed a star with naïve charm to make it a stage hit.

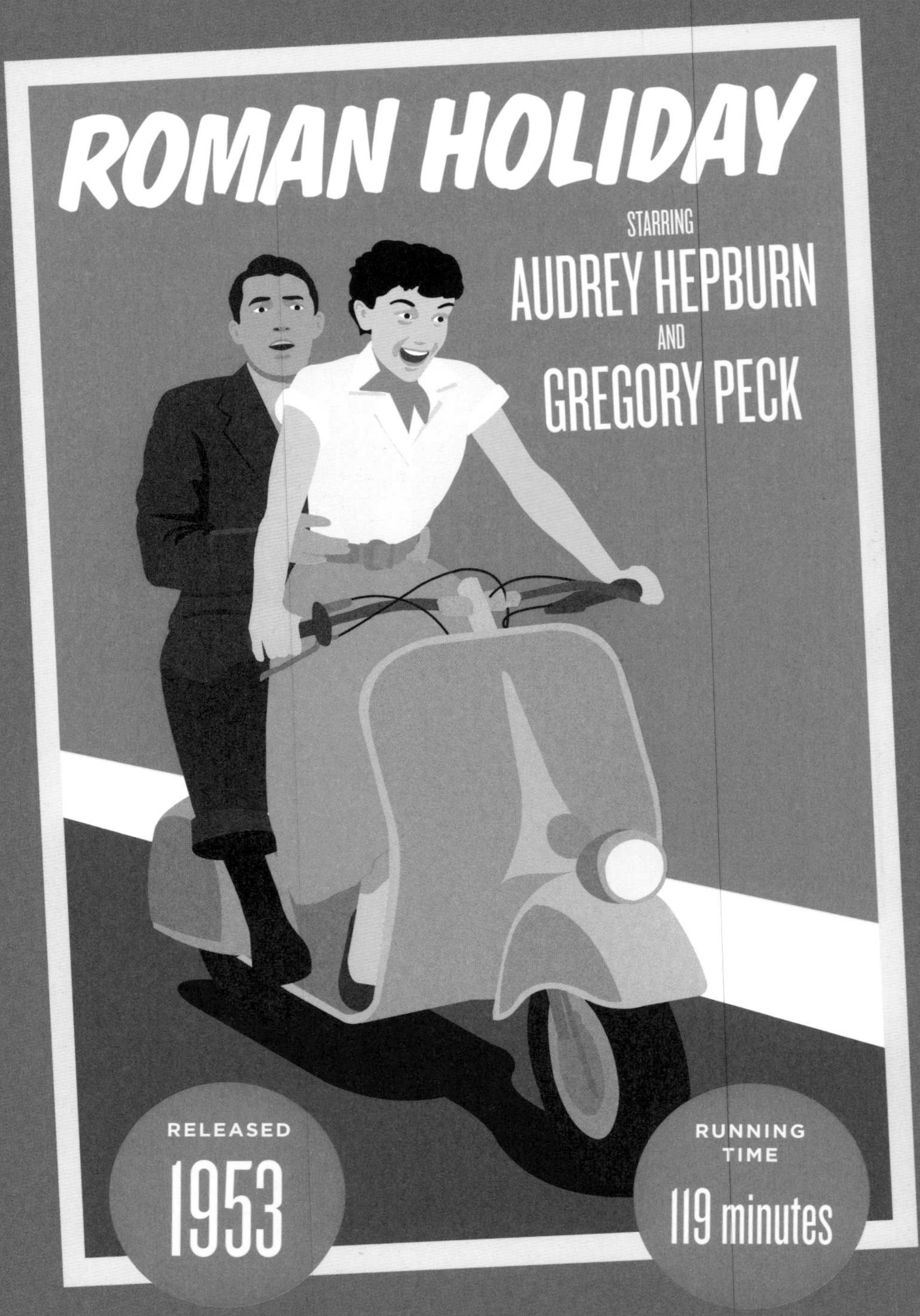

ROMAN HOLIDAY

STARRING
AUDREY HEPBURN
AND
GREGORY PECK

RELEASED
1953

RUNNING
TIME
119 minutes

The story of a royal princess who escapes from her gilded-cage existence and goes on the run in Rome was a perfect vehicle for Hepburn, who easily juggled the hauteur of royalty with the joy of an ordinary girl enjoying a day off in the Eternal City. Gregory Peck, playing a cynical journalist accompanying the princess gradually won over by her charm, offered a suave foil to Hepburn's enchanting performance.

MAIN CAST:

AUDREY HEPBURN
Ann, royal princess of a never-named country

GREGORY PECK
Joe Bradley, an American journalist working in Rome

IRVING RADOVICH
Eddie Albert, Bradley's photographer colleague

3 ACADEMY AWARDS

Best Actress, Best Costume Design and Best Story. It was nominated for seven more awards.

The Best Story award for *Roman Holiday* was accepted by Ian McClellan Hunter. He was fronting for the actual writer, Dalton Trumbo, who was blacklisted in America for refusing to give evidence before the House Un-American Activities Committee during the anti-communist purges at the time. Trumbo eventually received the award posthumously in the 1990s.

$1.5m
BUDGET

$12m
GLOBAL BOX OFFICE

The movie was shot in black and white because of a face-off between the director, William Wyler, and the studio, Paramount. The budget allowed either for colour or location shooting, so Wyler opted for a black-and-white movie shot in Rome at Cinecittà, rather than on Paramount's Los Angeles back lot.

500,000

Number of Vespa scooters sold between 1953 and 1956. The movie was credited with doubling the sale of Vespa scooters over the three-year period – this was more than had sold over the preceding six years in total.

THE WRONG GIRL

Roman Holiday may have introduced Hepburn to the movie-going public as a new leading lady, but it was the part of Holly Golightly in *Breakfast at Tiffany's* that cemented her image for posterity. Truman Capote, author of the original novel, was not a fan, however. He felt that only Marilyn Monroe could play Holly as he had written her. Despite Capote's sourness about the casting, Monroe had already indicated her lack of interest in the part (and it was offered to at least two other actresses) before Hepburn accepted it.

Audrey played Holly Golightly as a good-time girl rather than Capote's 'American geisha'.

Audrey was not Paramount's first, or even second, choice for the part: not only Marilyn but Shirley Maclaine and Kim Novak had also said 'no' to it.

Audrey was herself not convinced she was right for the part, but was talked into it by the film's director Blake Edwards.

Audrey was proud of her performance, because it was the part most unlike herself that she ever played.

FINDING THE PRIZE

When Holly and Paul finally make it into Tiffany's and have a Cracker Jack ring engraved for her, the scriptwriter hadn't envisaged the problems it would cause. Cracker Jack was marketed as 'candy-coated popcorn, peanuts and a prize', sold in a red-and-white striped box featuring the cheery Sailor Jack and Bingo the dog. The prizes ranged from tiny whistles and spinning tops to glittering base-metal rings and bracelet charms. Nothing on the packet told you which prize it contained. The props team had to trawl through 200 packets in the interests of authenticity. One recalled that they must have found "50 goddamn whistles" before they finally hit pay dirt and came up with a packet with a ring in it. In 2016, the days of prizes came to an end. Today, rather sadly, Cracker Jack bags offer a digital code to an app instead.

WAS HOLLY A CALL GIRL?

Her inventor claimed not. Capote, interviewed by *Playboy* magazine in 1968, helpfully defined his term 'American geisha'. He said, "Holly is not precisely a call girl. She [accompanies] expense-account men to the best restaurants and night clubs, with the understanding that her escort was obligated to give her... perhaps jewelry or a check... if she felt like it, she might take her escort home for the night."

Marilyn was advised not to take the part by her acting coaches, Lee and Paula Strasberg, who felt that playing 'a lady of the evening' would cheapen her reputation.

Marilyn had a background that was far more like that of the 'real' Holly – Lulamae Barnes – than Audrey's very European roots.

Instead Marilyn acted in *The Misfits* (right), which had been written for her by her husband, Arthur Miller.

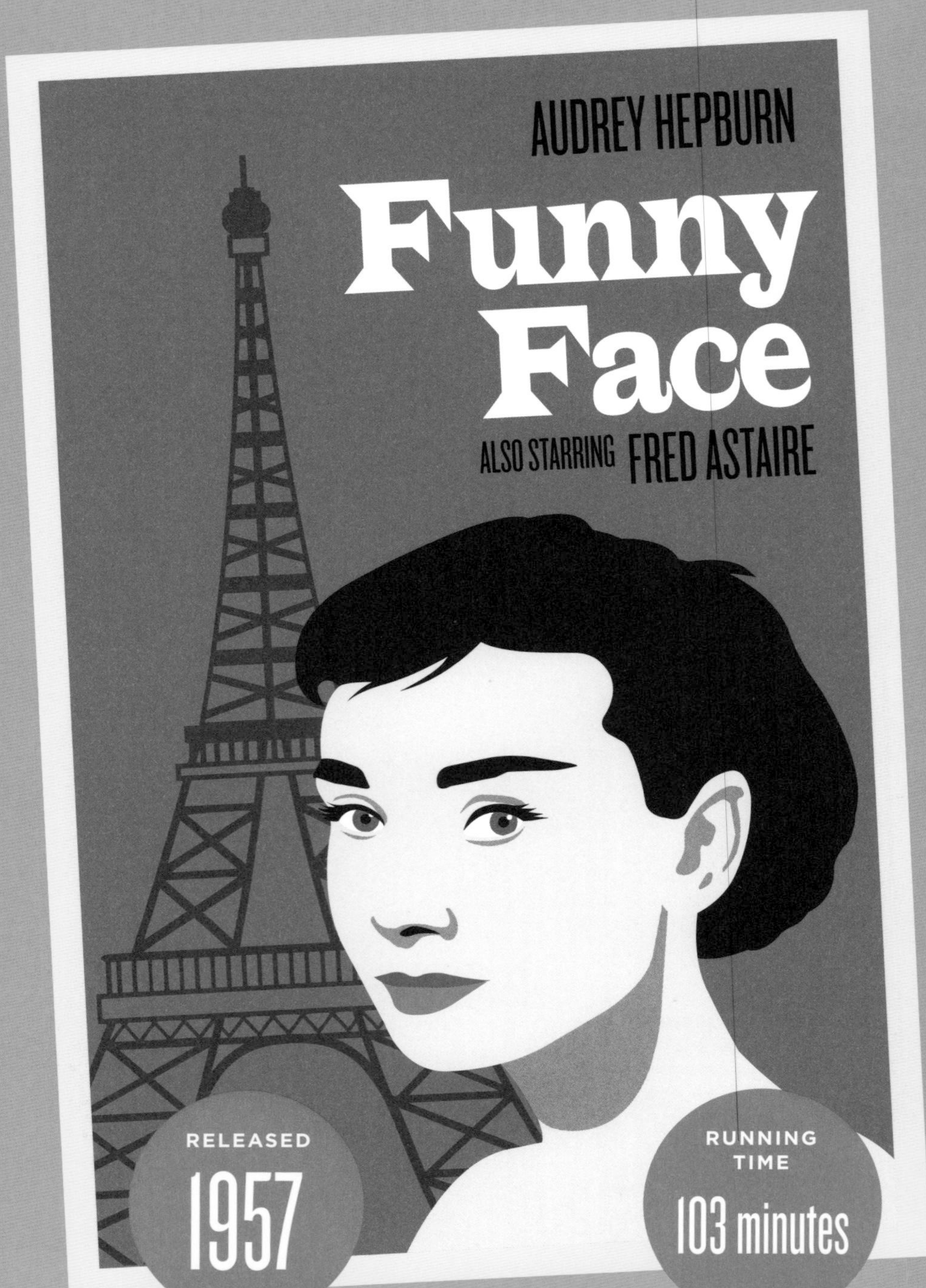

AUDREY HEPBURN

Funny Face

ALSO STARRING FRED ASTAIRE

RELEASED
1957

RUNNING TIME
103 minutes

Funny Face began life as a musical in 1927, composed by George and Ira Gershwin. By the time the movie of the same name was released 30 years later, almost the only things that had survived from the Broadway original were the male star – Fred Astaire – and four songs. The plot came from a show called *Wedding Bells* which was never produced, but the Cinderella role of shy bookshop assistant-turned-reluctant fashion icon was a natural fit for Audrey, and the film offered fans a satisfying blend of beatnik trends and high fashion against a Parisian backdrop, including all the major sights. Despite this, it had a mixed critical reception and was not a hit on release.

MAIN CAST:

AUDREY HEPBURN
Jo Stockton, bookshop assistant, amateur philosopher and unwitting model

FRED ASTAIRE
Dick Avery, celebrated fashion photographer

KAY THOMPSON
Maggie Prescott, editor of the high-fashion *Quality* magazine

7

Number of Parisian sights that are contained in the single musical number, 'Bonjour Paris': the Arc de Triomphe, the Champs Elysées, the Place de l'Opéra, the Rue de la Paix, the Ritz hotel, Sacré Coeur and, of course, the Eiffel Tower.

All three main stars were based on real-life characters: Dick Avery on Richard Avedon; Kay Thompson on the eccentric *Vogue* editor Diana Vreeland; and Jo Stockton on Suzy Parker, Coco Chanel's favourite model.

BUDGET

$3m

Constant rain in Paris caused the shoot to overrun and the eventual cost came in at closer to $4 million.

BOX OFFICE

?

Unknown. The movie was not a hit and was not thought to have broken even.

4 ACADEMY AWARDS NOMINATIONS

Best Costume, Art Direction, Cinematography and Screenplay. It didn't win any of them.

JUNIOR PARTNER

The age differences between male and female leads have often been a debated issue in the movies, and Audrey was not alone in playing opposite co-stars who were often old enough to be her father (or, in one or two cases, almost her grandfather). Even in the world of Hollywood where people were used to big age discrepancies, the matching of the girlish Hepburn with veteran stars such as Humphrey Bogart or Gary Cooper sometimes raised eyebrows.

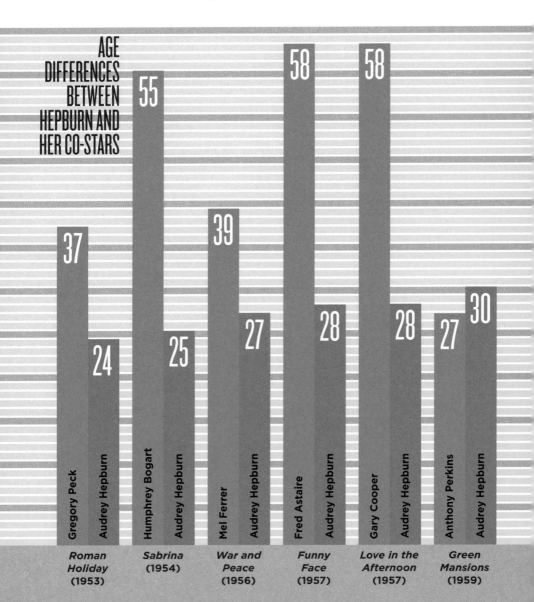

AGE DIFFERENCES BETWEEN HEPBURN AND HER CO-STARS

Movie	Male co-star	Age	Audrey Hepburn Age
Roman Holiday (1953)	Gregory Peck	37	24
Sabrina (1954)	Humphrey Bogart	55	25
War and Peace (1956)	Mel Ferrer	39	27
Funny Face (1957)	Fred Astaire	58	28
Love in the Afternoon (1957)	Gary Cooper	58	28
Green Mansions (1959)	Anthony Perkins	27	30

Over the 11 years covering most of her major hits – between *Roman Holiday* in 1953 and *My Fair Lady* in 1964 – the differences in age between Audrey and her leading men were, almost without exception, huge. Apart from *The Nun's Story* (in which her leading man could be said to be God – and therefore ageless), in only one case was a co-star younger. In total there were 187 years in age difference between Hepburn and her co-stars over 12 movies – brought down in one case by three years, due to the fact that Audrey's star in one of her few flops, *Green Mansions*, was Anthony Perkins, three years her junior.

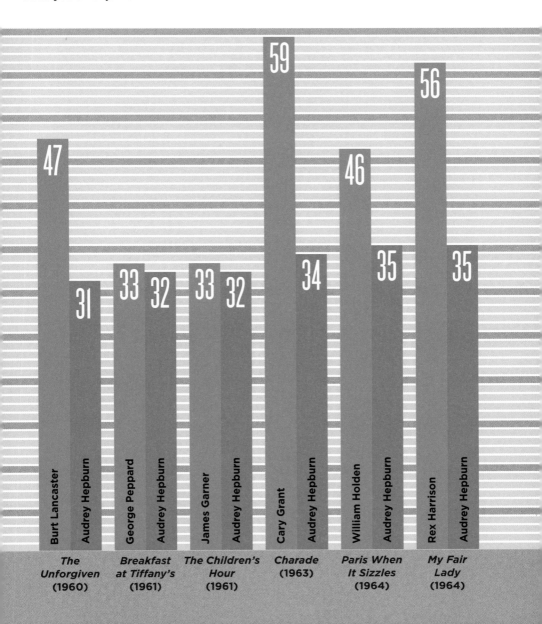

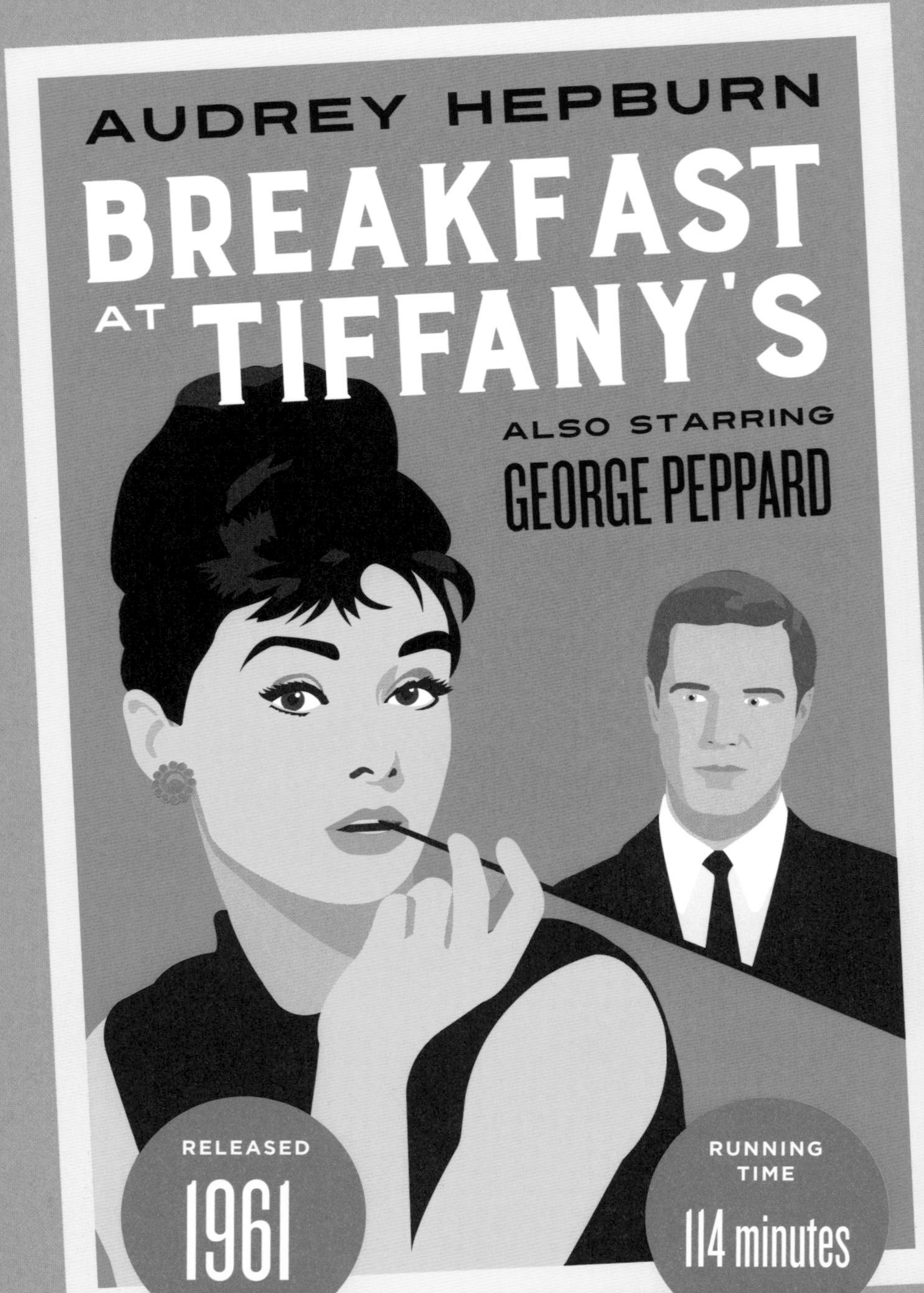

AUDREY HEPBURN

BREAKFAST AT TIFFANY'S

ALSO STARRING
GEORGE PEPPARD

RELEASED
1961

RUNNING TIME
114 minutes

The original author of *Breakfast at Tiffany's* may not have wanted Audrey to play Holly, but today it's the film for which she is probably best remembered and her most nuanced performance as a child bride from Texas reinventing herself as a New York society girl. Her style, from sunglasses to updos, and from cocktail frocks to men's shirts, was quickly absorbed wholesale into the 'look book' of want-to-be sophisticates and has never really gone away.

MAIN CAST:

AUDREY HEPBURN
Holly Golightly, a good-time girl

GEORGE PEPPARD
Paul Varjak, a struggling writer trying to make his way in New York

PATRICIA NEAL
Emily Eustace Failenson, '2E', a wealthy decorator

2 ACADEMY AWARDS

Best Score and Best Original Song – the latter for Hepburn's memorable performance of 'Moon River', by Henry Mancini and Johnny Mercer.

£467,200

The price made at auction for the little black dress, designed by Givenchy for the film's opening scene, sold at Christie's in 2006.

$2.5m
$8m

BUDGET   US BOX OFFICE

9

The number of cats who played 'Cat' in the movie. One was an established feline acting star called Orangey who won his second Patsy – the animal Oscars – for his work.

2005

The date of the first recorded protest against white actor Mickey Rooney being made up ('yellowface') to play the Japanese Mr Yunioshi, which makes uncomfortable viewing today. The film's scriptwriter, George Axelrod, suggested that the character was offensive and should be removed, but its director, Blake Edwards, insisted on keeping the role in.

ONE WORLD

Audrey was introduced to UNICEF in 1987 by her cousin, Leopold Quarles Van Ufford, then Dutch ambassador to Portugal – who invited her to speak on the organization's behalf about the effects of global poverty on children. With her lifelong concern for children and their wellbeing, her popularity, and an ability to speak powerfully and simply on subjects that moved her, Audrey was a natural fit for the cause. Between 1988 and 1992, she undertook eight gruelling journeys highlighting poverty, famine and disease all over the world. She had always looked delicate, but in the role of UNICEF's international goodwill ambassador, she proved she was tough.

Main trips Hepburn undertook...

MARCH 1988

ETHIOPIA

To draw attention to the poorest country in the world at that time, in the grip of famine and civil war.

AUGUST 1988

TURKEY

To gain support for an immunization programme in a country where infant mortality was very high.

OCTOBER 1988

SOUTH AMERICA (including Venezuela and Ecuador)

To raise consciousness of the plight of street children.

FEBRUARY 1989

CENTRAL AMERICA

To raise consciousness of mothers' and children's health issues.

APRIL 1989

SUDAN

To publicize Operation Lifeline, a project to get food to areas of Southern Sudan cut off by the civil war.

OCTOBER 1989

THAILAND / BANGLADESH

To draw attention to flooding, clean water shortages and threatening famine for poor children.

OCTOBER 1990

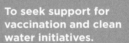

VIETNAM

To seek support for vaccination and clean water initiatives.

SEPTEMBER 1992

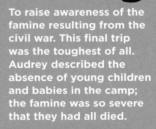

SOMALIA

To raise awareness of the famine resulting from the civil war. This final trip was the toughest of all. Audrey described the absence of young children and babies in the camp; the famine was so severe that they had all died.

"THERE IS A SCIENCE OF WAR; HOW STRANGE THAT THERE ISN'T A SCIENCE OF PEACE."

AUDREY
HEPBURN

MY FAIR LADY

ALSO STARRING
REX HARRISON

RELEASED
1964

RUNNING
TIME
170 minutes

FEBRUARY 1989

CENTRAL AMERICA

To raise consciousness of mothers' and children's health issues.

APRIL 1989

SUDAN

To publicize Operation Lifeline, a project to get food to areas of Southern Sudan cut off by the civil war.

OCTOBER 1989

THAILAND / BANGLADESH

To draw attention to flooding, clean water shortages and threatening famine for poor children.

OCTOBER 1990

VIETNAM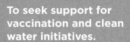

To seek support for vaccination and clean water initiatives.

SEPTEMBER 1992

SOMALIA

To raise awareness of the famine resulting from the civil war. This final trip was the toughest of all. Audrey described the absence of young children and babies in the camp; the famine was so severe that they had all died.

> "THERE IS A SCIENCE OF WAR; HOW STRANGE THAT THERE ISN'T A SCIENCE OF PEACE."

AUDREY
HEPBURN

MY FAIR LADY

ALSO STARRING

REX HARRISON

RELEASED

1964

RUNNING
TIME

170 minutes

My Fair Lady was a huge hit, although Audrey's performance wasn't universally admired. Being such an elegant and established star she had a hard time appearing convincing in the early scenes as a cockney flower seller – especially as, for once, she was old for the part she was playing: 30 to Eliza's supposed 19. Julie Andrews, who had played the part to great acclaim on stage, wasn't deemed well-known enough to carry a major film, and Audrey's singing was dubbed which, after sustained training to get 'in voice', felt like a wasted effort. Despite all this, *My Fair Lady* remains one of the great spectacles of 1960s musicals, and one in which Hepburn's style shone very brightly, aided by the design impresario Cecil Beaton's astounding costume design.

MAIN CAST:

AUDREY HEPBURN
Eliza Doolittle, a cockney flower seller

REX HARRISON
Professor Henry Higgins, an expert in phonetics

WILFRID HYDE-WHITE
Colonel Hugh Pickering, Higgins' long-time friend

8 ACADEMY AWARDS

Best Picture, Best Actor, Best Director, Best Costume Design, Best Original Music Score, Best Cinematography, Best Sound Mixing and Best Production Design. Audrey was not nominated for Best Actress.

$17m
BUDGET

$72m
GLOBAL BOX OFFICE

$400,000

The fee allegedly demanded by actor Peter O'Toole to play Higgins. It was deemed too high. Rex Harrison cost just $200,000 – against $1million earned by Audrey.

1,500

Number of costumes that Cecil Beaton is believed to have created for the film.

Filming of the 'Wouldn't it be Lovely?' number had just finished when news came of the assassination of President John F. Kennedy. George Cukor was too upset to tell his crew, so Audrey made an announcement to her colleagues.

FILMOGRAPHY

It may have seemed that Audrey's film career was an overnight success when she played her first lead in *Roman Holiday* – for which she won an Oscar – but she had already served her time in bit parts: it was her eighth film and she had been acting for over five years. Her film career was actually quite short, with all her major hits concentrated into a mere 14 years, although she continued to appear in movies until 1989, just five years before her death.

1948	Dutch in Seven Lessons	1951	One Wild Oat	1951	Laughter in Paradise	1951	The Lavender Hill Mob
1951	Young Wives' Tale	1951	Monte Carlo Baby	1952	The Secret People	1953	Roman Holiday
1954	Sabrina	1956	War and Peace	1957	Funny Face	1957	Love in the Afternoon
1959	Green Mansions	1959	The Nun's Story	1960	The Unforgiven	1961	Breakfast at Tiffany's

Hepburn clocked up 27 movies over her acting career, working with a remarkable number of leading directors, from Billy Wilder and King Vidor to William Wyler and Blake Edwards. After 1967, she appeared in only four more films, all rather undistinguished and with long gaps between each role. She stuck to her declaration that she never wanted to return to the movies full time.

1961 The Children's Hour

1963 Charade

1964 Paris When It Sizzles

1964 My Fair Lady

1966 How to Steal a Million

1967 Two for the Road

1967 Wait Until Dark

1976 Robin and Marian

1979 Bloodline

1981 They All Laughed

1989 Always

AWARDS

BAFTA

BAFTA NOMINATED

OSCAR

OSCAR NOMINATED

GOLDEN GLOBE

GOLDEN GLOBE NOMINATED

POLYGLOT AUDREY

Although she was famous for her linguistic abilities, Audrey had few chances to use them at work until she became an ambassador for UNICEF, when they proved invaluable both for travelling and in fundraising.

Audrey made two films in languages other than English. She spoke Dutch in *Seven Lessons*, 1948, a dramatized travelogue and her first acting role, and *Monte Carlo Baby*, 1951, which, unusually, was filmed first in English and then, subsequently, in French.

TALK TO THE ANIMALS

In *Green Mansions* Audrey exhibits the ability to talk an altogether different language – 'talking to the animals', rather like a waifish Dr Dolittle. The film would prove a rare box-office flop for her, but everyone agreed that her communication with her animal stars, including Pippin the fawn, was the most charming element in the movie.

AUDREY HEPBURN

04
LEGACY

"HOW SHALL I SUM UP MY LIFE? I THINK I'VE BEEN PARTICULARLY LUCKY."

—Audrey Hepburn, interviewed for the UNICEF charity

AN ELITE CLUB

Sadly, Audrey didn't live long enough to see her confirmed membership of one of the most exclusive clubs of people involved in the performing arts – she's an EGOTist: that is, someone who has won at least one each of the Emmy, Grammy, Oscar and Tony awards, for TV, recording, film and stage performances respectively. Audrey was awarded an Oscar in 1953 and a Tony in 1954. The Emmy and Grammy were awarded posthumously.

RICHARD RODGERS
**US COMPOSER
JOINED IN 1962**

HELEN HAYES
**US ACTRESS
1977**

RITA MORENO
**US ACTRESS
1977**

JOHN GIELGUD
**UK ACTOR
1991**

The oldest to reach EGOT status so far – at the age of 87

AUDREY HEPBURN
**DUTCH-BRITISH-IRISH ACTRESS
1994**

MARVIN HAMLISCH
**US COMPOSER
1995**

JONATHAN TUNICK
**US COMPOSER/
CONDUCTOR
1997**

MEL BROOKS
**US DIRECTOR
2001**

MIKE NICHOLS
US DIRECTOR/ PRODUCER
2001

WHOOPI GOLDBERG
US COMEDIAN/ ACTRESS
2002

SCOTT RUDIN
US PRODUCER
2012

ROBERT LOPEZ
US SONGWRITER
2014

The youngest to reach EGOT status so far, aged just 39

ANDREW LLOYD WEBBER
UK COMPOSER
2018

JOHN LEGEND
US SINGER/ SONGWRITER/ PRODUCER
2018

TIM RICE
UK LYRICIST
2018

At the start of 2019, there were just 15 official members, although there are a number of others who have just a single award left to win, including Cher, Martin Scorsese, Viola Davis, Lin-Manuel Miranda and Julie Andrews.

EMMY

GRAMMY

OSCAR

TONY

AUDREY AT AUCTION

Audrey gave many of her personal possessions away to friends during her last illness, and left others as bequests in her will. Most of the remainder was put up for auction by her sons in three major sales at Christie's London in 2017 and 2018. The items included were extraordinarily diverse, from powder compacts and scarves to personal correspondence and many, many pairs of the ballerina flats that were such a strong part of her image.

ESTIMATED SALES:
£650,000

TOTAL SALES:
£4.6m

TOP HIT!

SCRIPT FOR BREAKFAST AT TIFFANY'S
- £632,750

Audrey's personal working script for *Breakfast at Tiffany's* (including her own annotations and some deleted scenes) achieved the highest auction price for any script ever. It was bought, appropriately enough, by Tiffany's themselves.

Working script for *My Fair Lady*
£206,250

£10,625
Working script for *Ondine*, her Broadway success with Mel Ferrer.

Burberry trenchcoat £68,750

Givenchy black cocktail dress £60,000

Of the clothes Audrey wore in her films, the black Givenchy cocktail dress that was probably the most famous – made for her role in *Breakfast at Tiffany's* – was sold off at Christie's in an earlier sale, in 2006. It fetched $923,187, briefly holding the record for most expensive dress sold at auction ever until Marilyn Monroe's pleated white dress from *The Seven Year Itch* went on sale later in the year – and raised $5.6 million.

IN THE GARDEN

Once settled at her house, La Paisible in Switzerland, Audrey was a keen gardener, though her work absences meant that the large garden was also maintained by a gardener, Giovanni, who stayed with the household for many years. Fruit trees and a vegetable garden kept the kitchen supplied – she was particularly keen that there were always great bushes of basil plants ready to be harvested for pasta – but she also loved flowers. In recognition of her love of them, three were named for her.

DAY LILY

Hepburn's daylily, *Hemerocallis* 'Audrey Hepburn' is less restrained than her tulip or her rose: it's a frilly, pink-orange blend with golden edges to the petals.

TULIP

The Audrey Hepburn tulip is pure white and classically cup-shaped.

ROSE

The Audrey Hepburn rose is a delicate-pink hybrid tea with a light but persistent scent.

CELEBRITY ROSES

DOLLY PARTON
A frilly, light yellow-gold floribunda with a sweet, fruity scent

BARBRA STREISAND
A lavender hybrid tea rose with deeper-purple edges to the petals and a lemony scent

JUDY GARLAND
A deep orange-yellow floribunda tea rose with a golden heart

CARY GRANT
A bright-orange hybrid tea rose with a rich scent

INGRID BERGMAN
Deep, bright-red, double-bloom hybrid tea rose

ELIZABETH TAYLOR
Shocking pink, double-bloom tea rose

GINGER ROGERS
An orangey-pink hybrid tea with a 'true rose' scent

Audrey was far from alone when it came to roses. Many famous people have a rose named for them, and plenty of Hollywood stars were honoured with their own flower. Generally, it's intended that the flower has some match with the personality.

GRACE KELLY
'Princesse de Monaco', a cream hybrid tea rose with deep-pink margins to the petals

BING CROSBY
A pale-orange hybrid tea with a mild spice scent

DORIS DAY
A frilly, light yellow-gold floribunda with a sweet, fruity scent

TINA TURNER
A vivid-orange hybrid tea rose

GINA LOLLOBRIGIDA
A brilliant golden-yellow hybrid tea rose with huge flowers

MARILYN MONROE
A creamy-apricot hybrid tea rose with a light scent

8 THINGS YOU DIDN'T KNOW ABOUT AUDREY

AUDREY HEPBURN

USA 37

SHE'S ON A STAMP!

In 2003, her work for humanitarian causes was celebrated with a 37c stamp in the US. Another design, due to be issued in Germany in 2001, was destroyed when her son, Sean Ferrer, refused to grant copyright after the stamp had been printed – all but a few of the 14 million already printed were destroyed.

55 Audrey's lucky number was 55, as it appeared on the doors both of her dressing room on *Roman Holiday*, her first big hit, and her dressing room for *Breakfast at Tiffany's*. She asked the managers at the Studios de Boulogne in Paris if she could have the same number when she filmed *Paris When It Sizzles* – but her luck ran out and 55 failed to save the picture.

HAPPY BIRTHDAY MR PRESIDENT

One year after Marilyn Monroe sang Happy Birthday to John F. Kennedy in May 1962, Audrey did the same, but it was at a private party, and it wasn't recorded. It was to be his last birthday.

WEDDING GIFT

By the time she broke off her engagement to James Hanson in 1952, the wedding dress had already been ordered and made. She gifted it to Italian friends, asking them to find a poor Italian girl for whom it would be the wedding dress of her dreams.

FEAR OF WATER

She had a fear of water and was never a strong swimmer. *Two for the Road* featured a scene in which she had to be thrown in a swimming pool, and extras were placed by her side just out of shot, ready to boost her out of the water as soon as the shot was complete.

Audrey's favourite meal was spaghetti al pomodoro, made with homegrown produce, and including a large bunch of basil from the garden. She also confessed that her guilty pleasure was a 'piece of dark chocolate and a couple of fingers of whisky' after dinner.

DIAMONDS ARE FOR AUDREY

Hepburn was one of only two people who have worn the famous yellow Tiffany diamond, mined in 1877, and cut into a cushion-shaped brilliant weighing 128.54 carats. She wore it as part of the publicity for *Breakfast at Tiffany's*, in a necklace in which it was surrounded by diamond 'ribbons'.

PRINCESS LOOKS

Disney based the Briar Rose/Aurora character in *Sleeping Beauty* on Audrey's face and figure but gave her blonde 'Princess' hair.

LA PAISIBLE

Audrey's son Luca remembered her telling him that the reason she loved Switzerland so much was that there would never be a war there. When she found the house that would come to represent home for her last three decades, she was still married to Mel Ferrer, but she bought it in her own name and they lived there together only briefly. La Paisible was sold in 2000 and is now in private ownership.

MEANING:

'THE PLACE OF PEACE'

10 BEDROOMS

The 10-bedroom house was built in the 1700s, but had been substantially modernized by the 1960s.

TOLOCHENAZ

Located 15 miles west of Lausanne and 30 miles east of Geneva, but is itself a village with a population of fewer than 5,000 people.

After her death, the village square was renamed 'Place Audrey Hepburn'. In 2012 a bronze sculpture of her was erected on a plinth there.

SWITZERLAND

● LAUSANNE

Lac Léman

● GENEVA

FRANCE

LIFE AFTER DEATH

By the early 1990s, your death no longer placed a bar on your ability – or at least that of your image – to sell things. Increasingly convincing computer-generated images could be combined with body doubles and voiceover artists to convey the impression that a dead artist was right there selling you stuff. An advert that recreated Audrey was one of the more impressive examples of this trend.

1991 DIET COKE

Diet Coke were probably the first to jump on the bandwagon with their ads featuring contemporary celebrities mingling with long-dead ones: Elton John mixed with Louis Armstrong, James Cagney and Humphrey Bogart in one, while Paula Abdul enjoyed the company of Gene Kelly, Groucho Marx and Cary Grant in the second.

1997 COORS

Coors Light beer followed up with a 'John Wayne' ad: Wayne was a composite of a real impersonator and a degree of digitization, both of whom were thirsty for a Coors.

1997 DIRT DEVIL

Dust Devil vacuum cleaners came out with a Fred Astaire version the same year as Coors. Through the miracle of CGI, the legendary hoofer was seen dancing with a Dust Devil, and the ad was launched during a break in that year's Super Bowl. His widow had approved it; others, including his daughter, thought it a horrible desecration.

2013 GALAXY

Audrey is one of the most recent examples of posthumous advertising: she appears in an advertisement for Galaxy/Dove chocolate in which she seems to get off a bus, steal the driver's hat, place it on the head of a handsome young man driving in a convertible and settle herself down in the back seat to enjoy her longed-for chocolate. Made from a combination of computer graphics, two body doubles and literally millions of minute details copied from film showing the real 19-year-old Hepburn, it's almost unnervingly realistic.

Would Audrey have approved? Her estate gave permission; she herself was hardly in a position to object.

2016 GENERAL MOTORS

General Motors attached Albert Einstein's face to a model's body – on which 'E= mc²' is tattooed on the bicep. A judge in Los Angeles ruled that as it was more than 50 years since Einstein's death, his 'copyright' in his image had effectively run out – even though his estate disagreed.

$$e=mc^2$$

TYPOGRAPHIC AUDREY

PIPPIN
LA PAISIBLE
STYLE
ARNHEM
ELIZA
FUNNY FACE
GIGI
HIGH BUTTON SHOES

CINECITTÀ
OSCAR
ANIMALS
MARNI NIXON

GIVENCHY
ACADEMY AWARDS

AUDREY

MY FAIR LADY
WARNER BROTHERS
SEAN
FRANCE
HOLLYWOOD

LANGUAGES
DANCER
DIVORCE
CINECITTÀ

ACTING
UNICEF
SABRINA
ROME
GRAMMY

SWITZERLAND
FASHION

BIOGRAPHIES

Hubert de Givenchy
(1927–2018)
French fashion designer, who opened his own fashion house in 1952 at the age of only 25. As well as his long-term association with Audrey, which began when he dressed her for *Sabrina*, he was also known as one of the favoured designers of Jackie Kennedy.

Doris Brynner
(b.1931)
Born in Yugoslavia, Doris Kleiner moved to Paris in the 1950s. She modelled for Chanel and Pierre Cardin and married the actor Yul Brynner in 1961 – their daughter, Victoria was Audrey's godchild. Doris met Audrey in the 1960s and the two were lifelong friends.

Sean Ferrer
(b.1960)
The older of Audrey's sons, from her marriage to Mel Ferrer, Sean was raised in Switzerland, Rome and the US. He has worked as a film producer and director, as well as in film design and marketing. In 1994 he founded the charity, the Audrey Hepburn Children's Fund.

Mel Ferrer
(1917–2008)
American actor and director, and Audrey's first husband. The couple met through Gregory Peck, married in 1954 and divorced in 1967. He starred opposite her in *War and Peace* directed her in *Green Mansions* and produced another of her hits, *Wait Until Dark*.

Connie Wald
(1916–2012)
Virginia-born ex-model and socialite, Constance moved to California in 1940, marrying the movie producer Jerry Wald in 1941. Living in Beverly Hills, Wald kept open house, entertaining many Hollywood personalities, including Audrey with whom she was good friends.

Robert Wolders
(1936–2018)
Dutch actor who would become Audrey's final partner after the death of his first wife, the actress Merle Oberon. They were content to remain unmarried and were happily together until Audrey's death in 1993.

Luca Dotti (b.1970)

Audrey's younger son, from her marriage to Andrea Dotti, was born in Switzerland and grew up there and in Rome. He became a graphic designer, has written several books about his mother and is involved with the Audrey Hepburn Children's Fund.

Sean Connery (b.1930)

Best known for playing James Bond, Connery starred with Audrey in the movie *Robin and Marian*. Although the pair would not act together again, the French government awarded them both the *Commandre de l'Ordre des Arts et des Lettres* in 1987.

Andrea Dotti (1938–2007)

Italian psychiatrist and Audrey's second husband. The couple met in the year she divorced Ferrer, and married in 1969, after which it was her boast that she became a 'Roman housewife' for a number of years. The couple divorced in 1982.

Henry Rogers (1913–95)

Old-school publicist Rogers did much to promote Audrey in her early career. Eventually they parted ways when he tried to persuade Audrey to demand a fee for promoting her Givenchy scent, *L'Interdit*. They remained friends.

Capucine (1938–90)

Capucine, an actress and model, met Audrey when modelling for Givenchy and the two became friends. Today, she's best remembered for playing the wife of the hapless Inspector Clouseau in the *Pink Panther* movies.

Billy Wilder (1906–2002)

Legendary German-born Hollywood director who worked with Audrey on both *Sabrina* and *Love in the Afternoon*. He became long-term friends with Hepburn.

● friend
● family
● partner

INDEX